Which of the following were discovered or invented by kids?

a. Television
b. Pterodactyl fossils
c. Braille

Answer: All of the above!

These substantial contributions to science and many others were due to the efforts of children and teens—curious and smart kids who often started with only a simple idea or sketch. This book tells the stories of nine such kids, all of whom made lasting impacts in science, including lesser-known people like Philo Farnsworth, the teen inventor of television, and Mary Anning, the young girl who became one of the world's most renowned paleontologists. Each chapter is a testament to what young people can achieve through creativity, imagination, and persistence.

"Inspiring fare for budding inventors." —Kirkus Reviews

". . . a unique and enthusiastically recommended addition to any school or community library collection." —The Children's Bookwatch

VOYA Nonfiction Honor List 2004
Parents' Choice Recommended

The Kid Who Named Pluto

To Kara, Macky and Dee —M. M.

To Kjerstin, Torsten,
Solvej and Jensen —J. C.

First paperback edition published in 2008 by Chronicle Books LLC.

Text © 2004 by Marc McCutcheon.
Illustrations © 2004 by Jon Cannell.

Book design by Jessica Dacher.
Typeset in Profile, Blockhead and Blockhouse.
The illustrations in this book were rendered in pen and ink with collage.
Manufactured in China.
ISBN 978-0-8118-5451-1

The Library of Congress has catalogued the hardcover edition as follows:
McCutcheon, Marc.
The kid who named Pluto : and the stories of other extraordinary kids
in science / by Marc McCutcheon ; illustrated by Jon Cannell.
p.cm.
Summary: A collection of profiles of children and young adults whose scientific inventions made an
impact on the world, including Louis Braille, who discovered a way for the blind to read and write.
ISBN 0-8118-3770-X
1. Scientists—Biography—Juvenile literature. 2. Creative ability in science—Juvenile literature.
[1. Scientists. 2. Creative ability.] I. Cannell, Jon, ill. II. Title.
Q141.M146 2004
509.2'2—dc21
2003003662

10 9 8 7 6 5 4 3 2 1

Chronicle Books LLC
680 Second Street
San Francisco, California 94107

www.chroniclekids.com

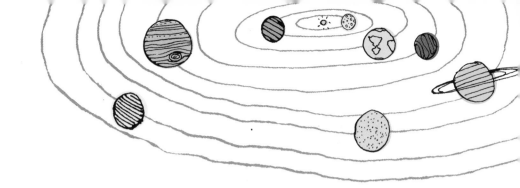

The Kid Who Named Pluto

and the Stories of Other Extraordinary Young People in Science

By Marc McCutcheon

Illustrated by Jon Cannell

chronicle books · san francisco

CoNTENtS

Introduction..11

The Boy Who Dreamed of Mars....................................13

The Girl Who Named Pluto..20

The Bookworm Who Became a Science Fiction Writer..............28

The Teenager Who Invented Television..........................37

The Curious Girl Who Discovered Sea-Monster Skeletons..........47

The High Schooler Who Created an Incredible Secret Code..........54

The Math Whiz Who Calculated the Movement of the Moon..........62

The Fourth-Grader Who Outsmarted Medical Experts..............69

The Blind Boy Who Developed a New Way to See..................74

Further Reading..84

Photo Credits..85

INtRODUCTiON

A 10-year-old uncovers a medical fraud.
An 11-year-old names a planet.
A 12-year-old discovers a rare sea-monster skeleton.
A 14-year-old invents television.

These are just a few of the amazing kids who have contributed to science, and contributed in a big way. Bright? Obviously. Creative? Absolutely. But beyond their intelligence and imagination, these kids had two things in common above all others: they believed in themselves and they worked hard. As the great American inventor Thomas Edison said, "Genius is one percent inspiration and ninety-nine percent perspiration."

Edison didn't believe genius was magical or mysterious. Instead, he believed it was just the result of plain old hard work. And who would know better? Edison had tried and failed with 1,000 different light filaments when creating the lightbulb, but he knew he would succeed if he kept on trying. By the light of our reading lamps, we can clearly see that he did!

This book is full of stories about remarkable kids who, like Edison, persevered—and had it pay off. As you read, you'll meet boys and girls who had great ideas and worked hard to make something happen with them. What are some of *your* great ideas?

one

The Boy Who Dreamed of Mars

In the late 1800s, five-year-old Robert Goddard wanted to fly. But unlike other boys, he didn't simply flap his arms and jump off chairs. He used science instead.

Having recently learned that electricity could make things move, Robert thought he would use it to fly. He held part of a battery, scuffed his shoes along the ground to create static electricity and launched himself into the air. Nothing happened. But he wasn't discouraged. His desire to reach the sky simply grew stronger.

Growing up in Roxbury, Massachusetts, in the 1890s, young Robert was often sick and missed more school than most kids. But his illnesses never slowed his imagination or his reading. One of the books he read was *From Earth to the Moon* by Jules Verne. At the time he read it, the notion of going to the moon was pure fantasy. Automobiles were just being introduced, and airplanes did not exist. But Robert saw some possibilities in Verne's far-out fiction. He scribbled notes in the book's margins, suggesting ways in which humans might actually be transported into space.

Robert's father, an inventor and businessman, was excited by his son's interest in science. To foster the boy's curiosity, he bought him a telescope, a microscope and subscriptions to science magazines. Robert set up a laboratory in his family's attic, where he conducted all sorts of experiments. He tried to make artificial diamonds, but a tube of hydrogen gas exploded, shattering glass onto the ceiling and doorway — but not forming diamonds. He flew the first box kite his neighbors had ever seen. And he directed his friends in digging a tunnel to China. (They spent a solid week at it before finally giving up.)

Robert also tried to build a *perpetual-motion machine*, a kind of motor that, once started, would become self-powered and never stop. But no matter how he configured it, he couldn't get it to work. (Robert didn't know that such a machine can *never* work because it actually breaks the laws of physics.)

Although many of his experiments failed, Robert learned a lot about science through doing them. At around age 16, he returned to his original fantasies of flight. He designed several flying machines on paper. When he finally came up with one he thought he could actually make, he bought some aluminum and set to work.

First, he pounded a very thin sheet of the metal into the shape of a pillow and cemented its edges together. He then inserted a valve, through which he pumped hydrogen gas from a tank. He hoped the gas, being lighter than air, would lift the vessel. With the help of a friend, he launched his flying machine from a sidewalk outside a nearby drugstore. But, as he wrote in his diary, "Aluminum balloon will not go up. Aluminum is too heavy."

In high school, Robert, still sickly and now two years behind in his studies, read another sensational book called *The War of the Worlds* by H. G. Wells. It tells of an imaginary invasion by martians who fly to Earth in iron spaceships. Robert wrote in his diary that the story "gripped my imagination tremendously." He read the book again and again.

Then, on October 19, 1899, Robert climbed his grandmother's cherry tree in Worcester to prune some branches. There a magnificent vision struck him. He later recalled:

> It was one of the quiet, colorful afternoons of sheer beauty which we have in October in New England, and as I looked toward the fields at the east, I imagined how wonderful it would be to make some device which had even the possibility of ascending to Mars, and how it would look on a small scale, if sent up from the meadow at my feet.

Robert would never forget this vision and in fact made October 19 a personal holiday, which he called "Anniversary Day." From that day forward, he made it his life goal to study space travel. He began by observing butterflies and birds to learn their secrets of flight. He took notes on how they used their tails to turn and how they could increase their speed by becoming more streamlined. He noticed that some birds cut through the air much faster than others, simply because of their shape. He also observed guns and cannons and explored how their firing ranges can be increased in various ways.

After much study, Robert wrote an article called "The Navigation of Space," which he sent to *Popular Science News* magazine. One of his central ideas was to use "the recoil of a gun placed in a vertical position with the muzzle directed downwards, to raise itself together with a car containing the operator." The magazine didn't publish his ideas.

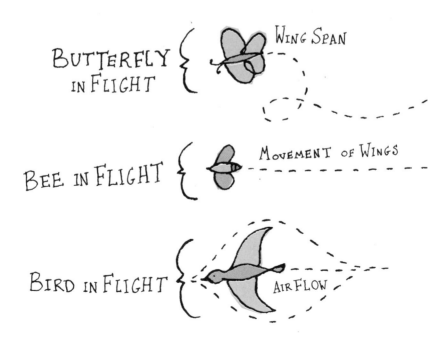

Soon after, Robert figured out that raising a 500-pound object to a height of 2,000 miles would require 56 tons of explosive! Using so much would be impossible. But no matter. His mind brimmed with other ideas. Robert graduated from high school and went on to study engineering at Worcester Polytechnic College.

In 1920, at the age of 38, Robert Goddard had an article published with the Smithsonian Institution, "A Method of Reaching Extreme Altitudes," which touched on the possibility of getting a rocket into space. But the *New York Times* ridiculed his ideas, saying he "lacked the knowledge ladled out daily in high schools." Space flight, they claimed, was impossible because there was no air in space for the rocket's motors to push against. (The truth is, as we now know, that a rocket's motors push against the inner walls of the rocket itself, not against space.) The paper was to apologize to Goddard posthumously 50 years later, the same month that humans walked on the moon for the first time.

In 1926, Goddard used liquid fuel to launch a homemade 10-foot rocket nicknamed *Nell* to a height of 41 feet. It landed in his aunt's cabbage patch 184 feet away after flying for just 2.5 seconds. "It looked almost magical as it rose," he later wrote.

Goddard went on to become one of the greatest aerospace engineers in history. Without him, America would not have landed the first man on the moon in 1969. Goddard successfully launched 35 liquid-propelled rockets in his lifetime. There were 23 additional flight tests in which the rockets did not lift off. But because of his determination and optimism, he called his failures "valuable negative information." He invented the multi-stage rocket, which links two or more rockets together in order to fly higher. He designed a rocket chamber and nozzle that produced a more powerful thrust, and he was the first to use liquid fuels instead of solid ones, for superior performance. All in all, he is credited with more than 200 inventions, most of them involving rockets.

Although Goddard died in 1945 at age 63, before seeing a human in space, today he is known as the father of space flight. NASA's Goddard Space Flight Center is named after him. And scientists say that his ultimate dream of getting humans to Mars—the vision he had in the cherry tree—may come true as soon as the year 2025.

mit of balloon; 20 miles

limit of atmosphere
200 mile

700 miles   -6 miles/s

1 lb

50 lls (H)

Robert Goddard at
Clark University, 1924

The Girl Who Named Pluto

At the Lowell Observatory in Flagstaff, Arizona, on February 18, 1929, an astronomer named Clyde Tombaugh couldn't believe what he was seeing. Through an eyepiece on a machine called a Blink-Comparator, Tombaugh examined two photos of the Gemini constellation. Each showed the same glimmering stars, but the pictures were not identical. The second photograph was taken a week after the first, and during that time something had changed. The astronomer saw that a tiny beacon of light — a mere pinprick — was in a different place in the second photograph than it had been in the first.

An unknown object was traveling across the solar system!

Tombaugh was certain it wasn't a comet or an asteroid — the light was too big. Nor could it be a star — stars were too far away to detect movement of this kind. The object could only be one thing: Planet X!

For years, scientists had hunted for Planet X, the ninth planet in the solar system. Odd disturbances in the orbits of the planets Neptune and Uranus

showed that a source of gravitational pull was nearby, and astronomers believed that this mysterious source *must* be a planet, but year after year, they were unable to spot it. Now Tombaugh had a photograph of it.

With Tombaugh's discovery, the Lowell Observatory faced a question: What should they name the new planet? One idea was to name it after the great astronomer Percival Lowell, who had spent much of his lifetime searching for Planet X. Lowell had died before Tombaugh made his discovery, but Planet X turned out to be very close to where Lowell had predicted it might be. On the other hand, many scientists felt that the planet should be named after a character in Greek or Roman mythology, to follow tradition. Mars is named after the Roman god of war, Mercury after the messenger god, Venus after the goddess of love and beauty. *Percival* or *Lowell* just didn't seem to fit.

On March 13, 1930, which coincidentally was Percival Lowell's birthday, the Lowell Observatory announced the great discovery. The public was enthralled. How big was the new planet? How far away was it?

Could it be seen without a telescope? Although many questions could not be answered right away, the question of what to name the new planet created an immediate clamor. Suggestions poured in from astronomers and citizens around the world.

One person wrote in to suggest the name *Zymal* because that was the last word in the dictionary and this was the last word on planets in the solar system. Another wrote, "Why have only one lady in our planetary system?" and suggested *Idana* to accompany Venus.

Nearly 100 different names were suggested in all, but the final decision was left up to the members of the Lowell Observatory. At first they favored *Cronus*. In mythology, Cronus was the son of Uranus and the father of Neptune — perfect, right? But Cronus had already been used to name a falsely identified planet years earlier. So to avoid confusion, the observatory decided against it.

The debate persisted for weeks. In coffeehouses and observatories all over the world, people discussed the possibilities and their favorite choices.

Which Name Would YOU Choose for a Planet?

These are just a few of the suggestions people made:

Apollo

Artemis

Atlas

Bacchus

Cronus

Diana

Erebus

Idana

Minerva

Osiris

Pax

Perseus

Tantalus

Tombaugh

Vulcan

Venetia Burney, 1930

As luck would have it, 11-year-old Venetia Burney of Oxford, England, had just learned in school about the eight planets and the mythological characters they were named after. The planets and their names fascinated Venetia for many reasons, but especially because, 40 years before she was born, her great-uncle, Henry George Madan, had named the moons of Mars: Deimos and Phobos. The naming brought a great honor to her family. Hearing about the discovery of the new planet, she began flipping through her books on mythology. Could she be as clever as her uncle and name a celestial body? Would anyone in Arizona listen to an 11-year-old girl halfway around the world?

After much study and thought, Venetia went to her father and told him she had found the perfect name for the new planet. He thought her idea was brilliant and offered to telegram her suggestion to the observatory in America. Nearly everyone who read the telegram agreed that Venetia's suggestion was a winner. Her name? *Pluto.*

FAsCiNATING FaCT:
Friends and family affectionately started calling Venetia "Plutonia" after she named the planet.

§ Pluto §

Pluto was the Greek god of the dark and distant underworld, and as the farthest planet from the sun, Planet X was certainly dark and distant. Furthermore, the god Pluto could make himself invisible, and Planet X had been frustratingly hidden for years. In mythology, Pluto was the brother of Jupiter and Neptune. And Pluto began with the letters PL, which would be a thoughtful tribute to Percival Lowell.

At the age of 11, Venetia was hardly a world-class astronomer or scientist, but that didn't matter—her choice was perfect. The observatory officially proposed the name on May 1, 1930, and it caught on almost instantly. A few mild objections were heard, but *Pluto* stuck and most astronomers agreed that it was well chosen.

Today, scientists marvel that Pluto was ever found. Decades later, when space probes were visiting the planets, they discovered that the disturbances that scientists thought they had seen in the orbits of Uranus and Neptune, the same ones that had caused astronomers like Percival Lowell to conclude there was a ninth planet to be found, never really existed. It had been a coincidence that Lowell formulated his Planet X prediction, and sheer luck that Tombaugh stumbled upon it.

Pluto is less than half the size of the moon and 3.5 billion miles from the sun (Earth is 91 million miles from the sun). No space probe has ever visited this tiny frozen sphere, but scientists at NASA say that someday one will.

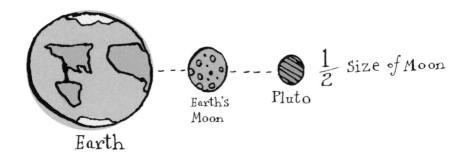

Earth

Earth's Moon

Pluto

$\frac{1}{2}$ Size of Moon

Pluto was thought to be the last planet in Earth's solar system, but in 2006 scientists redefined the term "planet," and Pluto didn't make the cut. Because it shares its orbit with other major objects, Pluto is now considered a dwarf planet, which means it isn't a planet at all. Whatever its classification, Pluto is not the last exciting discovery to be found in all of space. Scientists have recently found more than 100 new planets. Astronomers say that billions and perhaps *trillions* more are waiting to be discovered.

And who will name all those new planets? Although the planet's discoverer and the International Astronomical Union (an organization of astronomers) usually name new celestial bodies, anyone can make a suggestion—just like Venetia Burney.

FAsCiNATING FaCT:
Mickey Mouse's dog was named after Pluto one year after the dwarf planet's discovery.

PREPARE To NAME A PLaNET

Here are some steps to follow if you want to name a planet yourself:

• Visit the International Astronomical Union's website (www.iau.org) for its rules on naming new celestial bodies.

• Read science and astronomy magazines to learn about newly discovered planets. Visit astronomy websites to see what scientists are saying about new planets.

• Read Greek and Roman mythology and compile a list of the names you like, with reasons why they would make good celestial names.

• Read science fiction stories and classic works, such as those by Shakespeare, for other interesting names.

• Research which names have already been used to name new planets.

Note: So-called star registry companies will let you pay to register a name by computer, but this naming carries absolutely no legal weight. It is neither official nor internationally recognized by scientists or governments.

three

The Bookworm Who Became a Science Fiction Writer

A microscopic team of humans in a miniscule submarine cruises through the veins of a sick man's body.... A robot takes desperate measures to become human.... Citizens of an alien world panic as they witness their first nightfall in 1,000 years....

These are the plots of just three of the wondrous stories either written or co-written by Isaac Asimov, one of the greatest science fiction authors of all time. Asimov, who started writing at the age of 11, wrote in nearly every category—history, science, language, religion, geography, chemistry, ecology, math, mystery, reference, juvenile, humor—but it is his science fiction works that he is most famous for. Chances are good that you or somebody in your family has read a short story or book by Asimov or seen a movie based on one.

Few authors top him in sheer production, as he wrote nearly 350 books! And his scientific essays and science fiction stories have inspired numbers

of readers to become either scientists or science fiction writers themselves. So how did the young Isaac gain the ability and talent necessary to write so many books? What kind of childhood led him to imagine robots, space travel and life in the future?

Isaac was born in Russia in 1920, then was taken by his parents to America when he was three. He taught himself how to read at age four and began to write stories when he was 11. He graduated from high school at 15. Because his family was too poor to buy books, Isaac went to the local library. In his autobiography, he recalls himself at age nine:

> I read omnivorously and without guidance. I would stumble on books about Greek myths and fell in love with that world. When I discovered... the *Iliad* and the *Odyssey*, I took them out of the library regularly. I enjoyed them and read and reread them, often beginning again as soon as I had finished, until I had almost memorized them... I read Dumas and Dickens and Louisa May Alcott and, indeed, almost the entire gamut of 19th-century fiction.

Isaac read some books as many as 26 times! As most bookworms do, he preferred reading to any other activity. Because of this and because his parents needed him to work long hours in their candy store in New York, he spent little time with friends or playing like other kids. But it was in the candy store that he found the time to read. You might feel sorry for Isaac, but he didn't feel sorry for himself.

Although Isaac was a *voracious* reader, meaning no matter how many books he read it just wasn't enough, he didn't discover science fiction until he was 10. He stumbled upon the monthly magazines *Amazing Stories* and *Astounding Stories* and from the first few pages, was hooked. *Astounding Stories* was the best science fiction magazine of its day, and some of America's most imaginative writers contributed stories to it. The tales of aliens, robots and time machines so enthralled Isaac that he would often retell them to groups of fellow junior high students on the sidewalk outside of school.

FaSCiNAtING FAcT:
Isaac isn't the only science fiction writer to be published as a teenager. Robert Bloch sold his first story at 17. Greg Bear wrote his first story at age 10 and sold his first story at age 15.

Isaac not only read and reread every issue of these magazines (luckily, his father stocked them in the candy shop so he could read them for free!), he would also write to their editors and critique each story. Some of his letters were even published. As Isaac learned more about science fiction, he began to believe that he could write as well as some of the authors he was reading. Why not try?

Although Isaac had penned his first story at age 11, it wasn't until his mid-teens that he began to get serious. He then churned out a rapid succession of stories, which he submitted to the editors at *Astounding Stories* and *Amazing Stories*. His first dozen efforts were rejected, but Isaac persevered. He worked tirelessly at becoming a better writer. At 18, he wrote a story called "Marooned Off Vesta." It earned him the breakthrough he was waiting for — it was published in *Amazing Stories* a few months later, and

Isaac giddily collected his first writing check for $64 (approximately $820 in today's dollars). The rest, as they say, is history.

Asimov eventually sold nearly everything he wrote. This included short stories with such titles as "Ring Around the Sun"; "The Martian Way"; "I, Robot"; and "Stowaway." Today his short stories have been collected in no less than 33 volumes. Among his best works is a story entitled "Nightfall," which he wrote when he was just 20. The members of the Science Fiction Writers of America voted it the greatest science fiction story ever written.

One key to Asimov's popularity was his simple writing style; another was his attention to accuracy. Unlike many writers of his day, his science fiction had *real* science in it. When he wrote that the sun was 93 million miles away or that the sound of an explosion could not be heard in space, readers could be assured he was right.

While many authors describe their work as difficult — even agonizing — Asimov never did. He loved to write. He wrote as much as 18 hours a day, even when he was sick. He wrote on his birthday. He wrote on holidays. And it was this passion for his craft that made him so successful. At the peak of his career, he sold a piece every six days.

Isaac Asimov's career came full circle in 1976 when a new science fiction magazine was named after him. *Asimov's Science Fiction Magazine* is still being published today and is cultivating a whole new generation of award-winning authors. In 1987 he was given the ultimate recognition from his peers: the coveted Grand Master of Science Fiction award for his lifetime of achievements in the field. He died in 1992.

WANT TO BE A SCIENCE FICTION WRITER?

Before you begin, you should READ, READ, READ. If you want to write science fiction, you've got to love to *read* science fiction. So if you haven't already read a hundred or more science fiction short stories, this would be a good place to start.

Science fiction magazines are as popular today as they were when Asimov was a boy. These magazines pay writers, no matter what their age, for well-written stories. Two of the best are *Asimov's Science Fiction Magazine* (www.asimovs.com) and *Fantasy and Science Fiction* (www.sfsite.com/fsf). Once you have a story ready to send, write to the editors for their submission guidelines and follow them closely. These guidelines typically contain everything you need to know to professionally submit your story to the publication. Getting published takes time, so don't be discouraged if the first few stories you submit are not accepted. It's important to keep reading and writing science fiction to continually hone your science fiction writing skills.

Asimov holding science
fiction's coveted
Hugo Award, 1980

SCIENCE FICTION
ACHIEVEMENT AWARD
BEST NOVEL
OF 1979
THE FOUNTAINS
OF PARADISE
BY
ARTHUR C. CLARKE

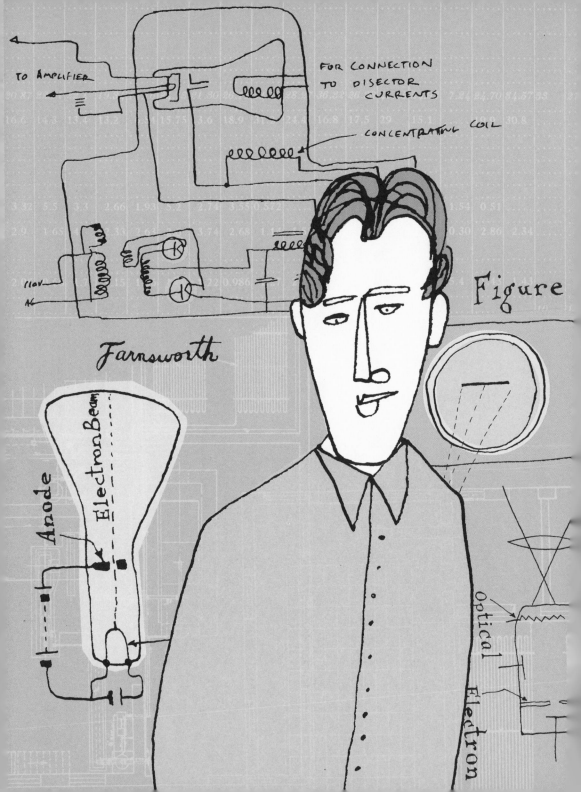

TO AMPLIFIER

FOR CONNECTION
TO DISECTOR
CURRENTS

CONCENTRATING COIL

110V
AC

Figure

Farnsworth

Anode

ElectronBeam

Optical Electron

four

The Teenager Who Invented Television

Philo Taylor Farnsworth grew up to be one of the most brilliant inventors of the 20th century. In fact, he made the first design for a television — when he was only 14 years old! Yet, unlike Edison with the lightbulb, or Alexander Graham Bell with the telephone, Philo is not commonly connected with the invention of television. Why has he been forgotten?

Philo was born in 1906 in Indian Creek, Utah. He grew up with four siblings, in a log cabin with no electricity. But Philo's father was always searching for better soil to farm, so in the spring of 1919, when Philo was 12, the family moved by covered wagon to a homestead in Idaho. As the wagon rumbled toward their new home, young Philo noticed something strange — there were wires strung between the different buildings of the farm.

"This place has electricity!" he shouted.

At that time, electricity was still new and wondrous. Philo thought it was the most amazing thing ever. When he watched it magically light up a room for the first time, it changed his life. And so did the stacks of discarded electrical and science journals he discovered in the attic of his new home. With the journals to guide him, Philo had the homestead's electrical system figured out within weeks.

When the family's generator broke down, it was Philo who got it running again. When he grew tired of hand cranking the washing machine (one of his many chores), Philo pieced together an electric motor to do the job. Then, one by one, he took his dad's farm devices and motorized those too.

His brother Lincoln, like many others, said Philo was "obsessed with electricity." His mother, Agnes, complained that his endless fascination with it interfered with his violin practice.

Usually a shy kid, Philo's confidence bloomed whenever he talked about his favorite subject. He loved to share his knowledge with others. In order to show how an electric current travels, for instance, he once lined up the members of his family and had them hold hands. Using low voltage, he shocked one person's hand, and everyone down the line felt the "tickle." When he was 13, he won $25 (approximately $350 in today's dollars) from *Science and Invention* magazine for his design of a thief-proof automobile ignition switch.

One day, when Philo had cocooned himself in the attic to study his science journals, an article jumped out at him. It was titled "Pictures That Could Fly Through the Air" and described a new concept called *Radiovision*. Since the 1880s, scientists had been trying to project images with whirling disks and mirrors. They believed that Radiovision would one day transmit both pictures and sound to screens in people's homes. It would be, they said, like a movie you could watch on a radio set. (Hugo Gernsback, a scientific publisher, was the first to call the concept *television*.)

Philo was thrilled by the prospect! In his mind, Radiovision (television) might indeed be possible, but not in the way the scientists were thinking. Philo realized that the disks and mirrors couldn't whirl fast enough to project an image, so he committed himself to creating a different concept.

At the age of 14, while Philo was plowing his father's fields, that concept struck him like a lightning bolt. The plowed rows under his feet formed a grid of lines, inspiring a revolutionary thought: Would it be possible to trap light in a jar and transmit it one line at a time on a magnetically deflected beam of electrons? As far as Philo knew, no scientist had ever proposed such a thing. Yet he believed it might be the very way in which a workable television could be built. From that day on, he told his family that he was going to "capture light in a bottle."

Philo persuaded his high school chemistry teacher, Justin Tolman, to tutor him before and after school. Philo asked Tolman endless questions about electricity. When Tolman ran out of answers, he let Philo explore his personal library. Tolman said Philo "devoured electrical encyclopedias like other students wolfed down popcorn." One day Tolman saw Philo drawing a series of electrical diagrams on his chalkboard. Puzzled, Tolman asked what he was doing.

figure No 3

electricity

"It's an electrical system for projecting an image," replied Philo.

"But what does it have to do with our chemistry assignment?"

"Nothing," Philo said. "It's my new invention."

Philo carefully explained the diagrams. Before long, Tolman believed that Philo's idea might actually work. But neither student nor teacher had the means to prove it. A device as complex as Philo had designed would cost thousands of dollars to construct. Tolman and Philo's family advised him to keep his idea secret for the time being.

A short time later, the Farnsworths ran into financial problems and moved to Provo, Utah. Then, when Philo was 18, his dad died of pneumonia. To help support his family,

Philo quit school and went to work installing and repairing radios. He also worked as a janitor, lumberjack and door-to-door salesman.

By 1925 Philo, who now called himself Phil, had become convinced that if he didn't build his television soon, someone else would beat him to it. Unfortunately, he was right. In New York, a brilliant Russian émigré named Vladimir Zworykin was developing his own ideas for electronic television. After many years of hard work, he was close to achieving his goal.

Philo Farnsworth, age 13

Phil Farnswoth needed a lot of money to make his invention a reality. While working as an office clerk, he decided to take a chance and reveal his plans to his bosses, two California businessmen named George Everson and Les Gorrell. His shy demeanor vanished, and Farnsworth was able to persuasively explain his vision. George Everson recalled in his biography:

> As the discussion started, Farnsworth's personality seemed to change. His eyes, always pleasant, began burning with eagerness and conviction; his speech, which usually was halting, became fluent to the point of eloquence as he described (the project) that had occupied his mind for the last four years.

The businessmen were bowled over by Phil Farnsworth's idea. They agreed to invest all of their savings, $6,000 (approximately $60,000 in today's dollars), in his first working prototype, and Farnsworth got to work. When glassblowers told him that the glass tubes he required were beyond their abilities, Farnsworth, with his good friend Cliff Gardner's help, made the tubes himself. Farnsworth's wife, Pem, did some of the spot welding.

For months the work continued 12 hours a day, six days a week. When the first prototype was finally completed, Farnsworth was ecstatic. But would it work? Pem Farnsworth described the scene:

> Les and George were all there for the big occasion, and Phil stood back and pushed the button and turned it on, and — BANG!... The power surge (from the) generator had blown the whole shebang, the tube and everything.

With his first television in shambles, Farnsworth had no choice but to go back to the drawing board. Only now he needed more money. Luckily, new investors were found who were willing to commit another $25,000 (approximately $250,000 today) to the project.

On September 7, 1927, in his San Francisco laboratory, Phil Farnsworth transmitted the very first television image in history. He turned on his new prototype, called an *image dissector*, and successfully transmitted a straight line onto his electronic screen. The following year, after Farnsworth had applied for a patent and had further improved the image's quality, on September 2, 1928, he announced his invention. The *San Francisco Chronicle* reported:

The laboratory model he has built transmits the image on a screen one and one-quarter inches square. It is a queer-looking little image in bluish light now, one that frequently smudges and blurs, but the basic principle is achieved and perfection is now a matter of engineering.

With news of Farnsworth's success, his rival, Vladimir Zworykin, paid him a visit in his laboratory. Farnsworth showed his brilliant peer everything. It was to prove a costly mistake.

Zworykin, who worked for the giant RCA corporation, improved on Farnsworth's designs. RCA offered to buy out Farnsworth for $100,000 (approximately $1 million today), but he refused. He knew there was much more money to be made than that. A patent war erupted: Zworykin and RCA claimed that they had invented television. But Farnsworth had the paperwork to show that he had done it first.

FASCINATiNG FaCt:
Farnsworth's image dissector, about the size of a quart jar, transmitted an image by cutting, or "dissecting," it into individual pinpoints of light. It then converted the pinpoints into a pulsating electrical current. The current, captured by a receiver, was then converted back into light to re-form the original image.

In 1934, the U.S. Patent Office settled the issue: it awarded priority of invention to Farnsworth. The design he had shown to his teacher back in high school had clinched it. As luck would have it, Tolman had kept the original diagrams.

Farnsworth signed a deal with Philco, the nation's biggest radio manufacturer, to build and sell television sets. But by 1936, only about 50 televisions had been purchased. The reason: there weren't very many shows to watch because the invention was so new. Baby Delores, a four-year-old singer and dancer, was one of the few entertainers on the air at the time. In fact, Farnsworth himself was so dismayed by television programming that he told his children not to waste their time watching it!

EARLY TELEVISION
PROTOTYPE

What meager television programming there was dwindled further during World War II, when television broadcasting almost came to a stop and commercial production of television sets was banned. It wasn't until after the war ended that the sale of televisions took off. RCA reportedly spent over $50 million ($500 million today) to develop the medium, and they credited Zworykin as the inventor. Farnsworth was forgotten as time went on.

Years later, in 1957, Farnsworth appeared on a television game show called *What's My Line?* The contestants had to guess his line of work and who he was. They didn't have a clue. He was one of the great geniuses of the 20th century, but virtually nobody recognized him. He died in 1971, all but forgotten by the public and frequently overlooked in the annals of great inventors.

Finally, in the 1980s, Farnsworth got his due. The U.S. Postal Service issued a stamp in his honor, and he was inducted into the Inventors Hall of Fame as the inventor of the first electronic televising device. In 1990 a statue of Farnsworth was erected in the Statuary Hall of the Capitol Building in Washington, D.C. The inscription reads, "Philo Farnsworth: Inventor of Television."

FASCiNATING FaCT:

Philo Farnsworth is credited with 165 different inventions. Most of them involve television and radio, but he also created a military radar system and the first enclosed, germ-free crib, called an Isolette.

five

The Curious Girl Who Discovered Sea-Monster Skeletons

Mary Anning grew up in the early 1800s as one of the unluckiest — and luckiest — kids around. Unlucky because she was born into poverty. Lucky because the cliffs near her home in Lyme Regis, England, held a treasure trove of fossils. Mary's father, a cabinetmaker who worked hard just to keep his family clothed and fed, was able to make extra money by finding these fossils, with the help of his children, and selling them to tourists.

In Mary's day, fossils were considered mysterious objects. Many believed that they were supernatural, crafted by God or the devil. But scientists were starting to uncover fossils' true origins. Soon it became known that fossils were the remains of prehistoric creatures — and the public became instantly fascinated with them. Scholars, museum curators and wealthy collectors clamored for specimens and gladly paid for them. People especially wanted those found at Lyme Regis, which was full of fossils from the Jurassic period.

When Mary was 11, her father died of tuberculosis. The tragedy plunged the family into despair. What would they do for money? How would they make a living without him? One possibility was obvious: the children could devote more time to fossil hunting. But searching for fossils along the beach and hanging cliffs of Lyme Regis was a dangerous job. Loose stones often tumbled down, crashing on the beach below. Entire walls of rubble would collapse unexpectedly. Mary's dog, her partner on many fossil hunts, was killed by such a rockslide.

Despite the danger and now without her father's guiding hand, Mary kept searching. She crawled along cliff faces. She scuttled over slick rocks. She waded through surf, even in the ankle-length dress she typically wore. And she uncovered many fossils. You see, Lyme Regis was a fossil hunter's dream. When the surf wasn't pounding at the cliffs, eroding the rocks and turning over new fossils, a cement company quarrying for limestone was stripping and chipping the cliffs away, exposing even more.

Mary quickly learned not only how to *excavate,* or carefully remove specimens without breaking them, but also how to clean, polish and mount the fossils like her father had done. As time went on, she even learned how to categorize the various bones and other objects she found.

On most days, Mary was happy to find ammonites (large spiral shells that once housed squidlike creatures), "devil's toenails" (mollusks that looked like the toenails of giants), petrified wood (wood that has turned to stone), crinoids (lilylike sea plants) and the imprints of ferns and fish, all of which she sold to tourists and collectors.

FASCiNATING FaCT:
The world-famous Ruth Mason Quarry in South Dakota contains the remains of nearly 2,000 duck-billed dinosaurs, called *edmontosaurs*. The quarry was named after the seven-year-old girl who originally discovered it.

But one day, when Mary was 12, she and her brother uncovered something amazing. Intrigued by a monstrous outline in the rocks, they clawed and chipped and eventually dug out a four-foot-long skull of what they thought was a crocodile. It took a year for Mary to uncover the other twenty-six feet of the skeleton, which she excavated herself.

The skeleton was later identified as an *ichthyosaur*. It was the first complete specimen the Geological Society in London had ever seen. (Mary would eventually find two more!) The ichthyosaur was a large reptilian predator with long jaws loaded with sharp teeth. It had been extinct for millions of years. The Annings made a quick and profitable sale, and the fossil was exhibited in William Bullock's Museum of Natural History in Piccadilly.

Some years later, Mary stumbled onto another big "first." This time, as she chipped and cleared away stone, from beneath her hands emerged not just a single bone or skull, but an entire skeleton of a bizarre creature she could only have imagined in nightmares. It had large fins similar to paddles and a body like that of a whale. But, unlike a whale, it had a long, serpentlike neck and a small head full of jagged teeth. Scientists called it a *plesiosaur.*

The skull of one of the ichthyosaurs
collected by Mary Annings from the Lower
Lias at Lyme Regis

Mary's plesiosaur generated such astonishment that many tales of sea serpents sprang from its discovery. Indeed, the Loch Ness monster in Scotland is said by some to be a surviving plesiosaur. Mary sold her specimen to the duke of Buckingham for a handsome price. Nearly two centuries later, it's still considered one of the most spectacular sea fossils ever found.

With the plesiosaur find, Mary's reputation as an amateur *paleontologist* (scientist who studies fossils) blossomed. She helped her family with the money she earned, and she helped scientists and scholars—and even the king of Saxony—who wanted to know just how she had found so many remarkable fossils. Many of them even joined Mary as she collected specimens along the beaches of Lyme Regis. Soon Mary's knowledge and experience grew beyond that of many professional paleontologists. As her reputation spread, she was called the "Princess of Paleontology."

Mary Anning made many great finds during her lifetime. One of the most remarkable came five years after she had discovered the plesiosaur. Once again, she must have been perplexed at what she saw under her fingers. This new fossil wasn't particularly large, but what it lacked in size, it made up with strangeness. For here was a reptile that appeared to have sprouted wings! Geologist William Buckland compared the fossil to one of the "dragons of romance and heraldry."

She had discovered the remains of a flying reptile, which scientists called a *pterodactyl*. Pterodactyl skeletons were extremely rare, and discovering this obscure specimen in addition to her previous rarities was almost beyond belief.

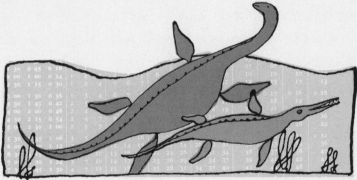

But her banner year had only just begun. Later that year, Anning uncovered the fossil of an octopuslike creature complete with an ink sac—that still had ink in it! A friend of hers, Elizabeth Philpot, actually used the ink—which dated back several million years—to sketch with. This new creature was called a *belemnosepia.* Before the year was out, Anning would find a fossil of a fish called *squaloraja,* a specimen that scientists then described as a cross between a shark and a stingray.

These would not, however, be the last great specimens Anning would discover. She found her third ichthyosaur in 1830. It was larger than her first find and ended up on display in the Natural History Museum in London. And that same year she discovered a second plesiosaur!

In 1838, at the age of 39, Mary Anning was formally recognized for her contributions to science when the British Association for the Advancement of Science granted her an *annuity* (yearly income). Soon after, she was made the first honorary member of the new Dorset County Museum for her life-long contributions to geology. Her success was all the more astonishing because she was doing something few other women did in the 1800s. At that time, fossil hunting was considered a man's job.

Today Mary Anning rests in a graveyard overlooking the cliffs and beaches where she spent so much time fossil hunting. Nearby there is a road named after her. The Philpot Museum, named after Elizabeth Philpot and her sisters, who also hunted fossils in the area, now sits on the site where Mary's house once stood, filled with information about her and the fossils she found on the cliffs and beaches of Lyme Regis. Some people even think that Mary is the "she" in the tongue twister "She sells seashells down by the seashore."

Perhaps the ultimate tribute to Anning came on the Easter of 2000, when fossil hunter Tony Gill found a 40-foot ichthyosaur skeleton, the largest ever discovered in Lyme Regis. He named the specimen Mary.

The High Schooler Who Created an Incredible Secret Code

Born in 1982, Sarah Flannery of Blarney, County Cork, Ireland, was, by all appearances, an ordinary girl. She grew up on a farm. She liked basketball, reading, playing the piano and talking to her friends. Only slightly out of the ordinary, perhaps, was her passion for mathematics. Many kids pale at the thought of algebra, calculus and trigonometry, but not Sarah. Since early childhood, she has loved the challenge.

Sarah's father is a mathematician who encouraged his children to borrow from his library of math books and kept a blackboard up in the kitchen on which he presented puzzles, or "maths" as the Irish call them, for his children to solve while dinner was being prepared. One of the first problems Sarah remembers solving was the Two Jars Puzzle, which her father posed to her when she was only five years old: Given a five-liter jar and a three-liter jar and an unlimited supply of water, how do you measure out four liters exactly?

16 CM

fill 5ℓ jar. Then use it to fill the 3ℓ
jar so there is 2ℓ left in 5ℓ jar.
Empty 3ℓ jar and pour the 2ℓ from
the 5ℓ jar into the 3ℓ jar. Fill up
the 5ℓ jar again and top up the 3ℓ jar
with the extra ℓ it made.

5ℓ

3ℓ

52103
210500
1102 579
5789

3 2 5 6 1 0
9 8 5 2 0 0 1 5
2 3 5 7 6 9
5 2 6 9 2

85 504 47 56 554 52 22
94 505 47 66 555 52 38
03 506 47 75 556 52 47
13 507 47 85 557 52 57
22 508 47 94 558 52 66
32 509 48 04 559 52 70
41 510 48 13 560 52 85
51 511 48 23 561 52 94
60 512 48 32 562 53 0
70 513 48 41 563 53 1
79 514 48 51 564 53 2
88 515 48 60 565 53 3
98 516 48 70 566 53 4
07 517 48 79 567 53 5
17 518 48 89 568 53 6
26 519 48 98 569 53 7
36 520 49 07 570 53 7
45 521 49 17 571 53 8
54 522 49 26 572 53 9
64 523 49 36 573 54 0
73 524 49 45 574 54 1
   55 575 54 2
   576 54 3
   77 54 4
   54 5
   54 6
   54 7
   48
   49
   0
   1
   2
   3

)-4 0-0 0-0 6-0 5-9 12-0 11-7 00 14 30-0 14 32-4 13 50-4 0-
)-6 0-1 0-1 6-1 5-9 12-1 11-8 01 14 30-3 14 32-6 13 50-6 0-
)-8 0-2 0-2 6-2 6-0 12-2 11-9 02 14 30-5 14 32-9 13 50-8 0-
-1 0-3 0-3 6-3 6-1 12-3 12-0 03 14 30-8 14 33-1 13 51-1 0-3 0-3
-3 0-4 0-4 6-   12-4 12-1 04 14 31-0 14   13 51-3 0-4 0-4
-6   5-5 12-2 05 14 31-3 14
   6 12-3 06 14 31-5 14
      12-4 07 14 31-8 14
      12-5 08 14 32-0 14
      12-6 09 14 32-3 14
   7 10 14 32-5 14
   11 14 32-8 14
   12 14 33-0 14
   13 14 33-3
   14 14 33-5
   15 14 33-8
   16 14 34-0
   17 14 34-

Sarah's answer:

> Fill up the five-liter jar. Then use it to fill the three-liter jar so that two liters remain in the five-liter jar. Empty the three-liter jar and pour the two liters from the five-liter jar into the three-liter jar. Fill up the five-liter jar again and use it to top up the three-liter jar with the extra liter it needs. Four liters now remain in the five-liter jar.

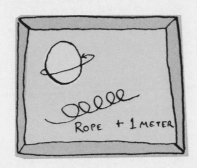

As Sarah got older, the problems posed by her father grew increasingly more difficult: Imagine a rope wound tightly enough around the earth that it fits as snugly as a wedding ring. Now make the rope exactly one meter longer, so that it's loose. How much space would be left between the encircling rope and the earth? Sarah answered: about 16 centimeters. She was right.

In 1998, when Sarah was 16, she won a national science fair with a project that explained *cryptography,* the science of turning information into secret code. Cryptography replaces each letter of an original message with another letter or symbol until an ordinary reader can no longer understand it. It is often used to protect top-secret diplomatic and military information, as well as everyday information such as credit card numbers and Internet passwords. Banks, businesses and governments all rely on cryptography to keep information safe from hackers, criminals and terrorists.

Sarah's father had many books on the subject and taught her that cryptography is created through complex mathematic formulas. Math is used to change, or *encrypt,* a message into code, and it's also used to *decrypt* the code back into an understandable message.

Sarah's science fair project was so impressive that she was invited to spend several days in a *workfare* project at Baltimore Technologies, one of the largest cryptography businesses in the world. Workfare assignments expose students to possible career choices. They are allowed to observe, or "shadow," employees and learn about their jobs. Often, students make coffee or perform menial tasks to help out while they observe and take notes. But Dr. William Whyte, the senior cryptographer at Baltimore Technologies, saw that Sarah was far too bright to simply sweep floors or make tea. He was impressed with her grasp of cryptography and showed her some of the new ideas that the head of the

company, Michael Purser, had been contemplating that involved encryption. He asked whether she could create a new code that incorporated some of those ideas.

It was an amazing request. To create a new mathematical formula, or *encryption algorithm,* that could code top-secret messages would require an immense amount of hard work and experimentation. Sarah would also have to learn some entirely new areas of mathematics. Could a teenager handle such a daunting task? It was intimidating, but Sarah was excited by the idea and accepted Whyte's challenge.

Her goal was to develop a new formula that would rival RSA, a standard worldwide system for encoding data that had been in use since the 1970s. Sarah formulated her ideas with painstaking care, writing out her blueprint on the same kitchen blackboard that her father had used to challenge her so many times before.

"I had a great feeling of excitement," she said about her assignment in *In Code: A Mathematical Journey,* a book she wrote with her father. "I think it was because I was working on something that no one had worked on before. I worked constantly for whole days on end, and it was exhilarating. There were times when I never wanted to stop."

But the job turned out to be harder than she had expected. "On one occasion very early on I had three laptops on the kitchen table all running different tasks." Sometimes, she said, "nothing was coming together."

Sarah Flannery and her father

But in time, Sarah managed to create a spectacular formula. It not only rivaled the standard RSA, it turned out to be 20 times faster! And as far as she could tell, it equaled the RSA in security. She didn't think it could be cracked by criminals. But could that really be true?

The idea that she had bested a standard, worldwide security system was almost impossible to believe. Certainly there must be a fatal flaw in her work, she thought. To find out, she entered her system in the annual international science fair sponsored by Intel. She called her project, "Cryptography—A New Algorithm versus the RSA."

The judges at the competition were stunned by the teenager's work, and so was the media. Her system could indeed encode a page of text 20 times faster than the existing system. Her project won first prize, and she was voted Young Scientist of the Year in Ireland and Europe.

WOrDS FROM THe CRYPT

The word *cryptography* comes from the Greek word *kryptos*,
meaning hidden.

Cryptography means hidden or secret writing and the enciphering
and deciphering of messages in secret code.

A *cryptographer* is a specialist in cryptography.

Cryptology is the scientific study of cryptography and cryptanalysis.

Cryptanalysis is the solving of cryptograms.

A *cryptogram* is a communication in code.

Sarah and her invention became front-page news. On the day after the contest, she had 65 calls from newspaper and TV reporters! She was approached by investors, some with millions of dollars to spend, who hoped to launch her invention in the marketplace. Attorneys urged her to patent her work and protect it from theft. Universities offered her scholarships. Businesses offered her jobs. Sarah was excited but overwhelmed.

But soon after the contest, a team of cryptographers managed to crack Sarah's secret code. Her system, it turned out, was fast — very fast — but not secure. And since security was far more important than speed, Sarah's system wouldn't be replacing the existing RSA. Still, she feels honored to have contributed something new and exciting to the world of cryptography. And perhaps someday someone will build on her work to create a new system that will dethrone the RSA. Perhaps that someone will be Sarah herself!

Sarah Flannery has traveled around the globe giving lectures on her work. Today she attends the prestigious Cambridge University. Who knows what she'll dream up next!

seven

The Math Whiz Who Calculated the Movement of the Moon

Child prodigy Truman Henry Safford was born in the village of Royalton, Vermont, in 1836. When he was just six years old, he asked his mother if she knew the number of *rods* (a rod is a unit of length equal to 5.5 yards, or 5 meters) there were around a certain meadow. He wanted to determine its circumference in *barleycorns* (an old unit of length equal to a third of an inch). His mother told him that there were 1,040 rods, and, with no paper or pencil to help him, Truman calculated the number in his head. In a short time he told his mother that the circumference was 617,760 barleycorns — he was correct!

How did the youngster accomplish this astonishing feat? Not with a calculator — they didn't even exist. Truman solved the problem with his own form of mental (and physical) gymnastics. Even at such a young age, he could multiply large figures in his head as rapidly as could be done on paper. At seven years old, he began to study algebra and geometry. He possessed astonishing powers of multiplication and concentration and became known as a *lightning calculator*.

In the 1800s, lightning calculators like Truman often went on the road to put on exhibitions for money, but Truman's parents, teachers with a high value on education, knew he was capable of doing better. And Truman himself wanted to do more than merely impress people. He wanted to achieve something—and he didn't want to wait until he was an adult to get started!

When Truman was nine, the Reverend H. W. Adams gave him an intense mental examination, posing mathematical problems like this for him to calculate in his head: Multiply 365,365,365,365,365,365 by 365,365,365,365, 365,365. According to Adams, Truman "flew around the room like a top, pulled his pantaloons over the tops of his boots, bit his hands, rolled his eyes in their sockets... and then, seeming to be in agony, said 133,491,850, 208,566,925,016,658,299,941,583,255!" The calculation had taken him less than a minute, and it was correct. (A modern handheld calculator can't even do this problem!)

It was only one of the many brain-draining questions Truman answered during the three-hour exam. He was also asked, What is the entire surface area of a regular pyramid whose slant height is 17 feet, the base a pentagon of which each side is 33.5 feet? In about two minutes, the boy gave his answer: 3,354,558 feet. Right again.

Then another: How many acres in a circular piece of ground with a circumference of 31.416 miles? The boy reportedly sprang to his feet, ran around the room, and answered, in about a minute, 50,265.5. He was right!

Dr. Chester Dewry, a mathematician who interviewed him, said, "He is a wonderful boy. His mind seems bent on the study of mathematics, and he takes his books about with him, that he may study some every day."

Also at nine, Truman researched, wrote and published his own almanac for Bradford, Vermont. The book contained tide tables; projected times for the rising and setting of the moon, sun and planets throughout the year; and other information, all of which had to be carefully calculated. Within the next year, he also created almanacs for Cincinnati, Philadelphia and Boston. One of his editions reportedly sold 24,000 copies!

In the mid-1800s, without the computers that today's astronomers rely on, formulating the positions of celestial objects was a complicated and time-consuming business. Truman found the process so slow that at age

Truman Henry Safford

10 he devised a new way to simplify the calculations. His system cut a quarter of the time it normally took to obtain moon risings and settings. He also formulated a new system to calculate eclipses in one-third the normal time.

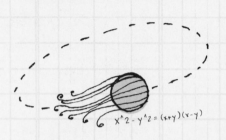

$$x^2 - y^2 = (x+y)(x-y)$$

At 14, he calculated the elliptical orbit of the first comet to appear in 1849. Later he calculated the orbital paths of several other comets. But Truman did not have a one-track mind. He also enjoyed chemistry, botany, philosophy, geography and history. He had an excellent memory and in school, as you might imagine, he advanced like a lightning bolt. He graduated from Harvard at the age of 18.

Almost at once he was hired to work in Harvard's observatory, making observations for a catalog that showed the locations of stars. In just a few years he became the observatory's director.

In 1865, at 29, Truman Safford was appointed professor of astronomy at the University of Chicago. During his time there, Willis Milham, a professor at a nearby college, recounted an anecdote where a student posed Safford with the following problem: "Suppose I was born at a certain hour, minute, and second of a certain day of a certain year. How old would I be in seconds at noon today?"

Professor Safford put his head slightly to one side in his characteristic way, walked up and down along the blackboard, and told him the answer.

"No," the student said to Safford, "that is not correct, for I have worked it out and the answer is different."

"What was your answer?" asked Safford. On being told, he again walked up and down along the blackboard and then exclaimed: "Oh! You forgot the leap years."

While a professor, Stafford also stood as director of the Dearborn Observatory. There he became fascinated with *nebulae,* the mysterious clouds of dust and gas that often surround newborn stars. He was immensely talented at finding them in the sky and discovered 103 new ones. He went on to publish star catalogs and to edit the annals of Harvard College Observatory. Safford died in 1901 at 65, but his descendants continued to sponsor astronomical studies for decades afterward, causing his legacy to live on even today.

No. 297

NEW YORK TIMES

the numbers were :

P. 59

JAMA

1.1.17.

A

Emily Rosa

R   L

47%   41

MODEL "B" FOLDER   MODEL "E" FO

8-9   9   8-9

EXPERIMENT

COURSE NO.   DAY   HOUR   DATE

OBSERVER   PARTNER

INSTRUCTOR'S SIGNATURE

A
B
C

eight

The Fourth-Grader Who Outsmarted Medical Experts

Nine-year-old Emily Rosa of Loveland, Colorado, grew up in a family of skeptics. While some skeptics focus their doubts on such things as psychic abilities, UFO sightings, witchcraft and fringe sciences, Emily's mother and stepfather were outspoken opponents of the medical treatment known as *therapeutic touch* (TT). So it was little wonder that when Emily needed a project for her fourth-grade science fair, she decided to disprove this treatment.

Therapeutic touch is practiced by thousands of nurses and physical therapists all over the world. Those who use it and many patients are convinced it works, but many people who watch the treatment take place are convinced it does not. Practitioners of therapeutic touch claim they can treat everything from arthritis to burns to cancer by simply moving their hands *over* a patient. The treatment begins by feeling a person's "energy field" and then using a special form of concentration to heal them. The procedure looks something like a massage, but the hands of the practitioner never touch the patient.

No scientific study has ever proven that therapeutic touch actually cures illness or that such a thing as a human energy field even exists. Yet many medical institutions pay therapists a lot of money to perform therapeutic touch on their patients. Is it science? Magic? Or only make-believe?

Emily thought it was make-believe, and set out to prove it. For her science fair project in 1996, she invited 21 therapeutic touch practitioners to participate in an experiment. She wanted to test whether they could really feel a human energy field. The therapists signed up — they were eager to prove themselves.

During the experiment, each practitioner sat across a table from Emily, who was hidden behind a cardboard screen, and stretched out their hands, palms up, through holes in the cardboard screen. Towels were draped over their arms on their side of the screen so they couldn't peek through the

DO YoU THINK YOU CAN FEEL SOMEOnE'S ENErGY FIELD?

Try it. Close your eyes and hold out your hands.
Ask a friend to hold his or her hands over yours without touching them.
Can you tell when they're there? When they're not?

holes. A coin toss determined whether Emily would hold her hand over the person's right hand or left hand. If practitioners could really feel someone's energy field, they should be able to sense which hand of theirs Emily's own hand hovered over. She ran the test twice.

When the experiment was over, Emily announced the results: In the first test, the practitioners had guessed right only 47 percent of the time. In the second, they were right only 41 percent of the time. The practitioners were upset! They started complaining that Emily's energy field was "off" or "weird." Some complained that they couldn't feel her energy because of her young age or because she wasn't ill. (Even though such therapists often practice by feeling healthy people's energy fields.)

Emily Rosa

The practitioners were further outraged when the results of Emily's test later appeared in the respected medical publication the *Journal of the American Medical Association (JAMA)*. While the *JAMA* editor called Emily's experiment absolutely "brilliant" and her methods "pure gold," the founder of therapeutic touch said she hoped the study's appearance in *JAMA* was an "April Fools' joke." *JAMA* was impressed by both Emily's test and by her performance. They met the standards of rigorous science, an amazing

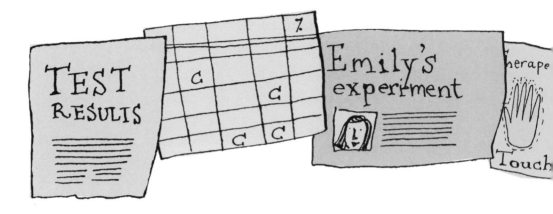

accomplishment for a nine-year-old. *JAMA* used Emily's experimental findings as well as their own to conclude that therapeutic touch claims "are groundless and that further use of TT by health professionals is unjustified."

The controversy caused by Emily's science project quickly caught the public's attention. News programs all over the world wanted her to talk about her findings on TV, and Emily found herself in whirlwind of publicity. She appeared on *The Today Show, Good Morning America* and on news programs on CNN, NBC, CBS, PBS and numerous local channels. She also appeared in such publications as *People, Time* magazine, the *Los Angeles Times*, the *New York Times*, the *Chicago Tribune*, and many more. Emily had made news. *Big* news.

Emily's experiment provided strong evidence that people cannot "feel" a human energy field, whether or not they think they can. But it did *not* prove absolutely that human energy fields don't exist or that therapeutic touch is useless

FASCINATING FaCT:

For Emily's next science fair project she will attempt to disprove "healing magnets," which some claim alleviate pain or cure illness.

for healing. In fact, many patients report feeling more relaxed and less stressed after a therapeutic touch session, and science has proven that people with less stress recover better from medical problems. Also, it has long been known that if a patient simply believes a treatment will work, it often will, at least a little.

nine

The Blind Boy Who Developed a New Way to See

One day, in the early 1800s in Coupvray, France, three-year-old Louis Braille wandered alone into his father's leather workshop and picked up an awl. It was perhaps the most dangerous of his father's tools and he had been strictly forbidden to touch it. Little Louis began to gash holes into a heavy piece of leather, just like he had seen his father do. At first it was great fun, but then something terrible happened. The boy's hand slipped, and the awl pierced his eye.

The doctor who was summoned to the house treated Louis's eye as best he could, but infection set in and then spread to Louis's other eye. Within a few days, Louis had gone blind. The boy was too young to understand what was happening to him. He asked his parents again and again, "When will it be morning again?" but nobody had the heart to tell him the answer. Louis would be blind for the rest of his life.

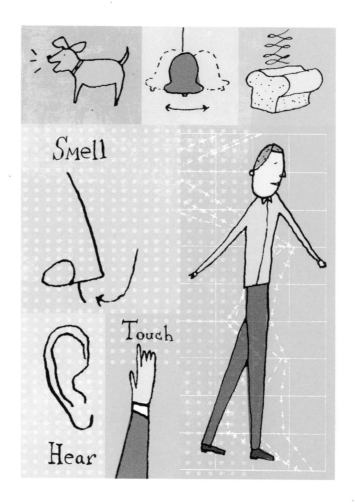

In the 1800s, blind children had few choices. They could not read, so most never attended school. As adults, they often became homeless beggars. Worried about their son's future, the Brailles taught him to do as many things as they could. His father showed him how to polish leather, which, to the boy's delight, he found he could do by touch. He learned how to weave leather fringes as well. To help Louis get around better, his father constructed a cane, which Louis could use to sweep the ground for obstacles in front of him.

As Louis got older, his parents gave him permission to walk to town alone. At first he got lost, but he soon learned how to tell where he was by touch, sound and smell. He knew, for example, when he passed the bakery by the heat of its ovens and the smell of its bread. The distinctive bark of a dog marked a particular house. The ringing church bells told him how close he was to the center of town. As his listening skills grew, Louis even learned how to identify neighbors and friends by the sound of their horse-pulled carts and wagons.

At the urging of a new village priest, Abbae Palluy, the local school-teacher agreed to try to teach Louis in his classroom. The youngster learned to do math in his head, but when it came time to read, he was lost. The Brailles knew how badly their son wanted to read, so when Louis was 10, they enrolled him in the Royal Institute of Blind Youth in Paris. That school used three-inch raised letters that blind students could "read" with their fingers. But Louis had difficulty mastering the raised print. It was easy to confuse the letters O, Q and C, the letters I and T, and the letters B and R.

Reading this way took so long that by the time Louis reached the end of a sentence, he'd forgotten what the first words were. To read a single book took him months of hard work. Raised-print books, which had to be made by hand, were so expensive the school library had only 14 of them. Wasn't there a better way? Louis wondered.

FASCiNATING FaCT:
Louis had a trick that helped him get around easier: he sang. When singing, Louis could listen for a very faint echo and actually determine how close he was to a wall.

In 1821 a military man named Captain Barbier informed the institute's headmaster, Dr. André Pignier, that he had invented a way for soldiers to send silent messages to one another in the dark. It was called *nightwriting*. His system used raised dots punched into paper by a tool called a *stylus*.

At first the students were excited by Barbier's system, but they soon found that it was hard to learn. It used many dots to convey a single sound and could not represent capital letters, punctuation marks or numbers. In the end, it was acceptable for communicating a single word, but it didn't work for an entire book.

Louis Braille "... to open the eyes of the blind." Isaiah 42:7

But the basic concept of Barbier's raised dots inspired Louis. Using a stylus, he began experimenting with raised dots of his own. After working for some time, an idea struck him. Why not create a system of raised dots not to convey sounds, as Barbier's system did, but to convey the 26 letters of the alphabet?

It seemed too simple to work. But when Louis began to tinker with the idea, he was electrified. He determined that the letter A would be represented by a single dot, the letter B by two dots aligned vertically, the letter C by two dots aligned horizontally, and so on.

Within a six-dot square—two across, three down—Louis could write 63 different letters, numbers and symbols.

When he demonstrated it to his blind friends, they were thrilled to discover that an entire letter could fit under a single fingertip. Now they could read and write! They could take notes in class. In fact, if someone came up with enough money, entire books could be constructed with Louis's system.

It wasn't long before the headmaster heard of Louis's invention and asked to see a demonstration. "Amazing!" he said, upon hearing Louis read from a paragraph of raised dots. As impressed as Dr. Pignier was, though, the school had no money to change its system and construct new books. When Dr. Pignier asked people for donations to help, they politely refused, not realizing what a critical difference the new system would make. Students adopted Louis's system for day-to-day uses, but it went no further.

At age 19, Louis became a teacher at the institute. He was much loved and respected

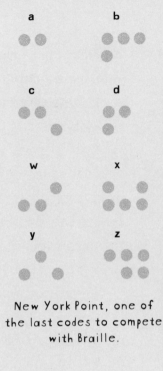

New York Point, one of the last codes to compete with Braille.

This is how Braille looks today.

because, unlike many others who taught in those days, he did not yell at, threaten or humiliate his students. "He used a firm kindness instead," an observer later wrote.

By this time, he had also become an accomplished piano player. Many thought Louis could have gone on to become a concert pianist, but he was determined to develop his alphabetic system and show other blind people how to use it. He spent his spare time constructing books for the institute. It was painstaking, tedious work.

Unfortunately, Louis got *tuberculosis,* a lung disease with no cure, and became very ill and weak. Under a doctor's care, he was able to regain some of his strength, however, and in 1829, when he was 20, he worked with Dr. Pignier to write and print a book titled *Method of Writing Words, Music and Plain-song by Means of Dots for Use by the Blind and Arranged by Them.* The book taught readers everything they needed to know about Louis's alphabet and reading system.

Dr. Pignier distributed copies to as many important people as he could. He hoped that someone with money and influence would be impressed enough by the system to invest in it, but the book was met with nothing

Early Braille typewriters

more than polite responses. Still Louis refused to give up. Even as his disease weakened him, he continued to tell people, even strangers, about his alphabet for the blind.

In 1841 Dr. Pignier left the school and was replaced by Dr. P. Armand Dufau, a harsh man afraid of change. When he learned of Louis's system, he scoffed at it, calling it "that silly punching of dots." Dufau went so far as to ban Louis's alphabet from the institute. Students were forbidden to use it in their classrooms, in the halls and on the grounds. He even burned all of the books Louis had worked so hard to construct for the school library.

Despite the ban, students continued to use Louis's system behind Dufau's back. When he took away their styluses, they used nails and knitting needles instead. The boys kept journals and passed notes to each other. No matter how hard he tried, Dufau could not control the entire school. Finally, a new teacher, Dr. Joseph Gaudet, convinced Dufau that it would be wiser to adopt Louis's system than to outlaw it. He said that one day, the system would be used everywhere. And wouldn't Dufau like to be a part of

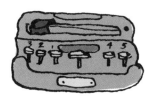  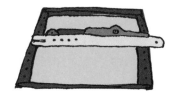

history? Dufau agreed, and once more the students could use Louis's alphabet whenever they wanted.

When a new school was built in 1844 to replace the aging, crumbling one, a demonstration of the alphabetic system was performed at the opening ceremonies. Some of the audience members thought it was just a trick. How could a blind person read so fast with his fingertips? Then a second demonstration, leaving no room for trickery, was performed, and this time the audience was convinced. What a wonderful new reading aid for the blind!

People began asking the institute about Louis's system, which was now being called Braille, and other schools began to adopt it. In 1884 the first Braille printing press was constructed and books using the alphabet system began to be mass produced.

Louis Braille himself, who had been forced to give up teaching in 1844 due to his illness, continued to make his own dot books for the school's library from his bed. But one day he was too weak to do even that. On January 6, 1852, he died at the age of 43.

By now there was no stopping the Braille system. The first school for the blind in America adopted the system six years after Braille's death. Within 30 years, nearly every school for the blind in Europe was using it. Today Braille is used worldwide.

A monument honoring Louis Braille was erected in his hometown in France in 1887. Five years later, his childhood home was turned into a museum. Even the leather shop where he was blinded has been kept complete with the original tools and accessories. A plaque out front sums up his life:

In this house on January 4, 1809, was born Louis Braille, inventor of writing in raised dots for use of the blind. He opened the doors of Knowledge for those who cannot see.

FURtHER READING

Brainstorm: The Stories of Twenty American Kid Inventors by Tom Tucker. Farrar Straus and Giroux, 1995.

I, Asimov by Isaac Asimov. Doubleday, 1994.

In Code: A Mathematical Journey by Sarah Flannery. Workman Publishing, 2001.

In Memory Yet Green by Isaac Asimov. Doubleday, 1979.

The Kids' Invention Book by Arlene Erlbach. Lerner Publications, 1999.

Louis Braille: The Boy Who Invented Books for the Blind by Margaret Davidson. Scholastic, 1991.

Mary Anning of Lyme Regis by Crispin Tickell. Lyme Regis Museum, 1996.

Thomas Edison: Young Inventor by Sue Guthridge. Aladdin Library, 1988.

We Were There, Too! Young People in U.S. History by Philip Hoose. Farrar Straus and Giroux, 2001.

PhOTO CREDiTS

MaRC McCUTCHeON is the author of *The Compass in Your Nose and Other Astonishing Facts About Humans* and 14 other books. He also owns Beach Books, a bookstore in Maine. He lives in South Portland, Maine.

JoN CANNeLL is the founder of Jon Cannell Design. He studied illustration, graphic design, and packaging at the Art Center of Design in Pasadena, California. He lives in North Bend, Washington, with his wife and three children.